THE ROLE OF
FEMALE
SPIES
IN
WORLD
WAR II

T0283696

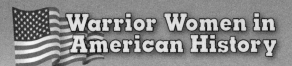

Warrior Women in American History

THE ROLE OF FEMALE SPIES IN WORLD WAR II

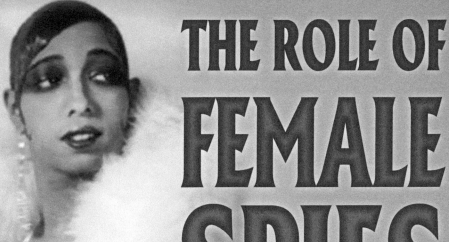

Cavendish
Square
New York

Hallie Murray

Published in 2020 by Cavendish Square Publishing, LLC

243 5th Avenue, Suite 136, New York, NY 10016

Copyright © 2020 by Cavendish Square Publishing, LLC

First Edition

Website: cavendishsq.com

This publication represents the opinions and views of the author based on his or her personal experience, knowledge, and research. The information in this book serves as a general guide only. The author and publisher have used their best efforts in preparing this book and disclaim liability rising directly or indirectly from the use and application of this book.

All websites were available and accurate when this book was sent to press.

Cataloging-in-Publication Data
Names: Murray, Hallie.
Title: The role of female spies in World War II / Hallie Murray.
Description: New York : Cavendish Square Publishing, 2020. | Series: Warrior
    women in American history | Includes glossary and index.
Identifiers: ISBN 9781502655493 (pbk.) | ISBN 9781502655509 (library bound) |
    ISBN 9781502655516 (ebook)
Subjects: LCSH: World War, 1939-1945–Secret service–United States–Juvenile
    literature. |
Women spies–United States–Biography–Juvenile literature. |
Espionage, American–History–20th century–Juvenile literature.
Classification: LCC D810.S7 M87 2020 | DDC 940.54′867309252 B–dc23

Printed in the United States of America

Portions of this book originally appeared in *American Women Spies of World War II* by Simone Payment.

Contents

Introduction

World War II, which lasted from 1939 to 1945, was the culmination of years of mounting tension across Europe and Asia that resulted in countries across the world grouping together into two major sides: the Allies and the Axis. Like World War I, World War II was what is known as a total war—the normal "rules" of war didn't apply. Every resource each nation had was entirely directed toward the war effort, and no one was safe. Civilians could be targeted just as easily as military fighters at the front, and citizens of nations across Europe lived in fear of bombings and other attacks. By the end of the war, fifty million people had lost their lives, hundreds of millions more were injured, many cities were severely damaged, and countless homes were destroyed.

The causes of World War II are numerous, but many can be traced directly back to the end of the First World War, which lasted from 1914 to 1918. In 1919, the Treaty of Versailles was signed, effectively ending World War I, with Germany forced to accept most of the responsibility for the war. Because of its role in the conflict, Germany was forced to pay significant sums to the war's victors, including England and France. These fines created even more issues for Germany's economy, which was already suffering because of the international depression of the 1930s. The

Adolf Hitler, pictured here in 1940, was a forceful speaker whose impassioned body language and intonation during speeches greatly affected his listeners and, in many cases, convinced German citizens of his viewpoints.

treaty also forbade Germany from creating a large army and enacted other restrictions that made Germans feel particularly resentful of other European countries.

Because of these difficulties, Adolf Hitler and the Nazi Party were able to gain power quite quickly. Before it became clear that Hitler was a genocidal autocrat, many Germans approved of him because he created policies that significantly bolstered the economy. As power became more centralized and Hitler's true goal of creating a German ethnostate became clear, most of the German population was either too scared to resist his policies or just didn't care as long as their families and livelihoods remained safe. Hitler blamed others for the depression that had a stranglehold on Germany. He promised to improve the economy and resurrect Germany as a military force. His ideas and passionate speeches sparked much of the German population. By 1933, Hitler was firmly in control in Germany, and by the late 1930s, it became clear that his ultimate goal was European domination.

World War II is usually said to have begun with Hitler's invasion of Poland on September 1, 1939. German airplanes bombed cities, roads, and airports, quickly rendering the Polish military helpless. In just a few weeks, Germany completely controlled Poland and thousands were dead. England and France declared war on Germany a few days later, and soon many other countries had united with England and France. This collection of countries fighting against Germany became known as the Allied powers.

At this time, the fascist dictator Benito Mussolini was in control of Italy. Japan was at war with China in its quest to overtake all of Asia, but it was facing major economic issues. Soon, Germany, Italy, and Japan had banded together and were known as the Axis powers.

The Axis attacks and invasions continued throughout 1939 and 1940, and many European countries fell to Germany. By June 1940, Nazis had occupied France, and by September 1940, Germany had begun bombing England. In June 1941, the Germans moved east, invading Russia.

Though the war began in September 1939, the United States wasn't officially involved until December 1941. Before then, the country had supported the Allies by sending supplies and resources, but America wasn't actually involved in the fighting. That all ended on December 7, 1941, when Japan launched a surprise attack on the United States and bombed the naval base at Pearl Harbor, Hawaii. A day later, the United States declared war on the Axis powers.

The war began to turn in the Allies' favor in early 1943, as Germany became weaker and the Allies won key victories in Europe and Russia. By January 1945, the German army was nearly destroyed, and on April 29, 1945, Hitler committed suicide. Germany officially surrendered a few days later. But the war wasn't over. Victory had been declared in Europe, but the United States and other Allied powers continued to fight Japan in the Pacific. Finally, in August 1945, World War II officially came to an end after America dropped atomic bombs on the Japanese cities of Hiroshima and Nagasaki. It was over. The Allies had won.

Throughout history, spies have played a key role both in war and peacetime. Often underestimated, women have participated in these espionage efforts, whether by

The front page of the *New York Times* from Monday, December 8, 1941, alerts readers of the Japanese bombing of Pearl Harbor, Hawaii, that occurred on the morning of Sunday, December 7.

smuggling supplies under skirts, developing relationships with military officials, or simply chatting with those in the know and gaining their trust. In the United States, women acted as spies in both the Revolutionary and Civil Wars, but it wasn't until World War II that they were officially commissioned by the government to help gather and analyze secret intelligence. And they often did so at great personal risk, taking on daring missions to help their country—"Few men showed greater courage, bore greater responsibilities, or took greater risks," writes one historian.[1]

Prior to World War II, the American government wasn't interested in using spies and assumed it could rely on the information gathered by its allies. But as the conflict in Europe escalated, it became increasingly clear that America needed its own organized intelligence agency, and quickly. In 1942, President Franklin D. Roosevelt established the Office of Strategic Services (OSS), the predecessor of today's Central Intelligence Agency (CIA).

Unlike the military, which was primarily made up of men, the OSS utilized women extensively. Members of the OSS needed to be intelligent and hard working. Some acted as spies, but others held different roles, including translators, map readers, code breakers, or telephone operators, all positions that could just as easily be filled by women as by men.

Working with the OSS and other intelligence agencies could be just as dangerous as fighting at the front. Women spies had to complete dangerous missions, sneak into prisons and government buildings, befriend and sometimes seduce powerful people, and brave the bombings and threat of military invasion that dogged all civilians in Europe during the war.

Women made up a large portion of the cryptographers and code breakers working for the Allies. This American cryptanalyst uses a contraption with alphabet strips on sliding scales to decode a hidden message.

Despite these dangers, women joined the OSS because they believed in the Allied cause and wanted to fight for their country, just as men did.

In the years since World War II, women have continued to work as spies for the US government. At the CIA, the official US spy agency, women hold all kinds of jobs, many serving in high-level positions. In fact, the CIA received its first female director in 2018, when Gina Haspel was named to that position. Although the tools of the trade, such as computers and high-tech gadgets, have changed, some things haven't: the bravery, intelligence, and spirit of these women have been invaluable to the United States.

The Limping Lady

Virginia Hall, nicknamed the Limping Lady of the OSS because of her artificial leg, was one of the most wanted Allied spies by the Gestapo, the German secret police. They called her "Artemis" and allegedly considered her the most dangerous of the spies working for the Allied nations. Hall worked behind enemy lines in France, first for Britain, and later on for her home country of America. Along with reporting key clandestine information back to Britain and France, she helped coordinate the activities of the French Underground, contributed to sabotage efforts in preparation for the Allied attack on D-Day, and helped connect the French Resistance with British and American supplies. Hall was honored for her service by all three countries—Britain, the United States, and France—and became a CIA analyst after the war, specializing in the workings of the French government.

Life Leading Up to the War

Hall was born to a wealthy family on April 6, 1906, in Baltimore, Maryland. She did well in school and was particularly interested in learning languages. She was very active, loved sports, and was president of her high school class. Hall spent summers on her family farm, learning about and playing with animals. She didn't know it at

This image of Virginia Hall was taken circa 1943 while she was working for Britain's Special Operations Executive, a secret organization formed to spy on and sabotage the Axis powers in Europe.

the time, but this knowledge of farm animals would prove especially useful in her later work as a spy.

Hall attended Radcliffe and Barnard College, where she studied French, Italian, and German. After college, she was ready for adventure and went to study in Vienna, Austria, and later in Paris, where she became very skilled at speaking French. Returning to Washington, DC, in 1929, she continued her studies at George Washington University but was soon itching to get back to Europe. In 1931, she began working at the US Embassy in Warsaw, Poland, and would later work at embassies in Turkey and Austria.

It was in Turkey that Hall lost her leg. During a hunting trip, she accidentally shot herself in the foot. Before long her wound had become severely infected, and her leg had to be amputated just below the knee. Hall was fitted with an artificial leg and from then on walked with a limp. However, during her long career in espionage, she "expected and received no special favors or allowances because of the artificial limb."[1]

Hall continued working as a secretary at American embassies in Europe, but eventually she wanted to get a better job at the US State Department. Unfortunately, the State Department didn't hire women or anyone with an amputated limb. Hall quit working for the government in 1939. She was frustrated with being stuck in an office, and even if the State Department disagreed, she didn't consider herself handicapped.

She then traveled around Europe and found herself in Paris when World War II broke out. Wanting to help the war effort, Hall began working at the French Ambulance Service. Hall believed that "after 12 years in Europe, it was her battle as well as that of her friends."[2] After it fell to Germany in June 1940, France became a dangerous place to live, and Hall was forced to go to England. There she found work at the US Embassy in London.

Working with the SOE

While working at the embassy, Hall became known to the British spy agency, the Special Operations Executive (SOE). It learned of her French language skills and familiarity with France. People at the SOE also believed Hall "possessed the courage, energy, self-confidence, and cool judgment [they] were looking for" and decided to recruit her.[3] Soon Hall was training for her new life as a spy. She learned how to work with weapons, how to operate radios and other communication devices, and how to organize groups that would try to resist Germany and take back France.

By August 1941, Hall was ready to be sent behind enemy lines. She would be the first SOE woman in the field. If Hall was nervous, she did not show it. She planned to pose as a reporter for the *New York Post*. The United States had not entered the war at this point, so American citizens like Hall still had the freedom to travel through France.

From her base in Lyons, France, Hall began gathering information while posing as a journalist. However, her cover as a journalist did not help her for long. With the bombing of Pearl Harbor in December 1941, the United States entered the war. As an American, Hall had become an enemy of Germany. She was now forced to operate in secret, steering clear of both French officials and Nazis occupying France.

Behind Enemy Lines

Hall was too resourceful to let this new situation slow her down. She was still able to pick up important information in bars and restaurants around Lyons. Hall was very friendly and motherly, and while she posed as a Frenchwoman, German soldiers would tell her all about their military jobs and missions. Hall would quickly feed that information back to the SOE office in London.

In addition to gathering information, Hall also helped Allied pilots who had been shot down over France. She smuggled them and other Allied prisoners of war (POWs) out of France. Additionally, she set up safe houses, secret places where agents could base their operations in the underground fight against the Nazis. Hall recruited French citizens to help her and her fellow agents in the fight. Eventually, the Nazis became aware of Hall's work with the French Resistance. The Nazis soon issued these orders: "The woman who limps is one of the most dangerous Allied agents in France. We must find her and destroy her."[4]

Conditions in France were becoming more dangerous by the day. In November 1942, Hall was again forced to leave the country. She found a Spanish guide to help her and a few other agents make the difficult trip across the Pyrenees Mountains into Spain. They faced cold weather and dangerous conditions, and Hall had a particularly difficult time dealing with her wooden leg. During the trip, she sent a message to the SOE office in London saying that "Cuthbert" was giving her trouble. The agent who received the message replied that she could have Cuthbert "eliminated." Little did he know, Cuthbert was Hall's nickname for her wooden leg!

Despite all of their precautions, Hall and others in her group were arrested at the Spanish border and sent to prison. There, Hall shared a cell with a Spanish prostitute. When the prostitute was released, she smuggled out a letter from Hall and sent it to the US Embassy in Barcelona, Spain. Finally, after six weeks in prison, Hall was released and went back to work, this time in Madrid, Spain.

From Madrid to Rural France

In Madrid, Hall was once again using a job as a newspaper reporter as a cover. This time, she was supposedly working for the *Chicago Times*. Her real job was to set

up a new network of agents and safe houses. Hall had become so used to danger that she found Madrid boring and the job too easy. In November 1943, she reported to

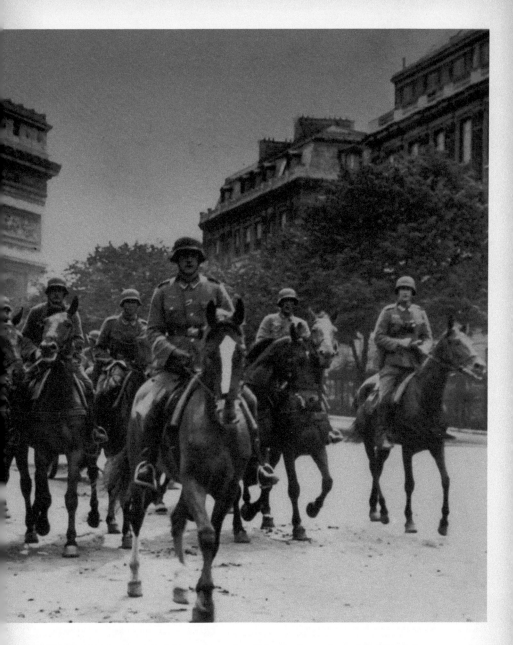

Nazi German troops ride on horseback in Paris on June 18, 1940, four days after the German occupation of France began and eight days after the French government abandoned the city.

Members of the French Resistance learned to use and maintain weapons, including pistols and revolvers, that were dropped off by parachute for their use.

England for additional training. There, she learned more about operating radios and how to prepare a parachute for a jump.

While she was training, she decided to begin working for the American OSS rather than the British SOE. Hall was given the code name Diane, and in March 1944, she was sent back into France. To make it less likely that the Germans still occupying France would detect her, she was carefully disguised. Her brown hair was dyed gray, and she wore heavy clothes to make her look plumper. She carried her radio transmitter tucked into an old, beat-up suitcase, and her forged papers identified her as a French citizen. She even disguised her distinctive limp by swinging her bad leg when she walked.

La Résistance

The French Resistance, known simply as La Résistance in France, was an underground organization that fought against the Nazi occupation of France, which began in June 1940. Early resistance efforts were scattered, but soon they began to become more organized through the efforts of the British SOE and the French secret service, which largely supported the Allies despite technically belonging to the Vichy government. Small groups of the French Resistance operated in cells that participated in guerrilla warfare against the Nazis, gathered information, and maintained newspapers that argued against Nazi propaganda. They also organized rebellious actions like strikes and sabotage. The French Resistance largely became obsolete when France was liberated from German control, but its legacy lives on.

Hall knew she would have to avoid major cities in France because German officers were everywhere. She then set up her new operation in central France. She called on friends who had helped her during her first stay in Paris, and within six months she had recruited and organized three hundred agents to carry out missions against the Germans. She trained them, got weapons for them, and communicated with the OSS office in London.

Needing safe places to make her radio transmissions, Hall found a series of farmhouses to use as her base of operations. She had to move often to stay one step ahead of the Germans. Sometimes she stayed with French families and would set up her radio in the barn or in an attic. Between July 14 and August 14, 1944, Hall sent thirty-seven radio messages to London. She reported on where the German army was located and arranged for airdrops of food, money, radio equipment, medical supplies, and soap for the Resistance fighters.

During the day, Hall worked as a milkmaid or goat herder, using skills from her childhood experience with the animals on her family's farm. These jobs allowed her to gather information as she delivered milk to local customers. She could also scout locations for the airdrops of supplies while working in the fields. At night, Hall would go to the prearranged airdrop location and wait for the supplies.

The Germans' Retreat

By early fall 1944, the Germans were being chased out of France by Allied forces. To help the Allies, Hall trained a new group to make things as difficult as possible for German troops remaining in France. Hall's group blew up bridges, destroyed German communication lines, and

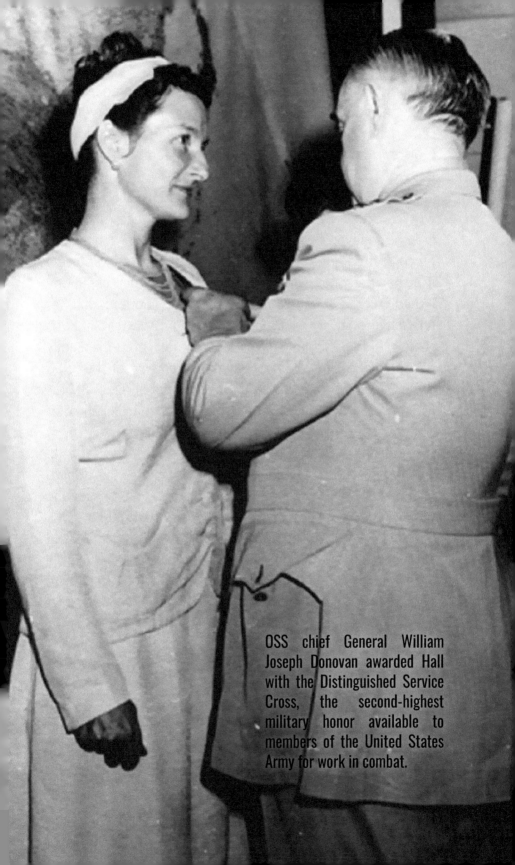

OSS chief General William Joseph Donovan awarded Hall with the Distinguished Service Cross, the second-highest military honor available to members of the United States Army for work in combat.

captured troops whenever possible. They are credited with capturing about 500 Germans and killing 150 others. During this time, Hall also met her future husband, Paul Goillot, a fellow OSS agent who had been born in France but was raised in New York City.

Hall's work during the war was valued highly, and she was awarded the Distinguished Service Cross, an honor that had never been given to a woman or nonmilitary officer before. President Harry S. Truman wanted to present it to her personally, but Hall thought an award ceremony would call too much attention to her and interfere with her future undercover work. She sent a message from Paris saying, "No, I still have work to do here."[5] Hall eventually accepted the medal in a private ceremony at the OSS office in Washington, DC, on September 27, 1945. Major General William "Wild Bill" Donovan, the director of the OSS, presented the medal.

After the war, Hall continued to work for the OSS. In 1947, the OSS became what we now know as the Central Intelligence Agency (CIA). Hall continued to work for the CIA in Europe until 1951, and then in Washington, DC. She quickly advanced at the CIA, and during the Cold War she helped the United States prepare for a possible war with Russia. In 1966, Hall finally retired and lived near Baltimore until her death in 1982.

An American in the Philippines

Claire Phillips was an American spy who spent most of World War II in the Japanese-occupied Philippines. After her husband was captured, Phillips disguised herself as a dancer, hoping she might be able to locate information that would help her rescue him. Unfortunately, he passed away in a prison camp, but Phillips stayed in the Philippines to help the American war effort by collecting information from Japanese officers who frequented the cabaret club she owned. She also worked with other Americans and anti-Japanese guerrilla fighters to smuggle supplies to American prisoners of war. In 1944, Phillips was captured by the Japanese military and imprisoned, where she suffered torture and months of solitary confinement until finally being freed by American forces in January 1945.

The Philippines at the Start of the War

Claire grew up in Portland, Oregon, and as a young girl she was "crazy about the theatre."[1] She left high school to tour with a traveling entertainment show as a singer and dancer. All through her twenties, she traveled around the United States and abroad before returning to Portland. There she was briefly married and had a daughter, Dian.

Claire Phillips is greeted by Major Kenneth Boggs and a Women's Army Corps honor guard on arriving back in the United States in 1951. Major Boggs was a prisoner of war in the Philippines whose rescue by the Allies was a direct result of Phillips's espionage activities.

After her divorce, in 1941, she decided to take her young daughter with her to Manila, in the Philippines, where Claire had been while on tour and had made friends. With World War II already raging in Europe, Claire and Dian arrived in the Philippines in September 1941, just a few months before the United States entered the war.

Soon after she arrived in Manila, Claire got a job singing in the Alcazar Club. It was there that she met a young American radio operator, Sergeant John Phillips. They fell in love and almost immediately began making plans to get married. Before they could, Japan attacked Pearl Harbor, and a day later, on December 8, 1941, the United States declared war on Japan. Soon, American citizens were no longer safe from the Japanese troops invading Manila. Claire went to the bank and withdrew all her money, bought medicine and food, and filled her suitcases with things she and Dian would need.

By the middle of December, Claire and John decided that she should take Dian into the hills outside Manila to escape bombings that had begun in the city. John's military unit was also based in the hills, so he and Claire were able to see each other from time to time. Claire and John weren't sure when they might be separated, so they decided to get married on Christmas Eve, 1941. After the wedding, they were able to spend a few hours together before John had to return to his military camp. Days later, the small village where Claire and her daughter were living was bombed. Claire had to say goodbye to John, and although neither of them knew it at the time, it would be the last time they would see each other.

Escaping Japanese Forces

During the winter of 1942, Claire Phillips and her daughter continued to hide in the hills, living with Filipino families that were hiding from the Japanese armies. They had very little to eat, living on rice, sugarcane, bananas, and occasionally some animals they were able to trap. They had to deal with snakes and rats and serious illnesses like malaria.

That winter, Phillips heard that there were American soldiers living on a nearby mountain, and she decided to go to their camp to see if one of them might be John. She made the journey to the American camp but was disappointed to see that her husband was not there. She did meet an American soldier named John Boone, who suggested that Phillips could help them by returning to Manila to gather supplies. Phillips knew it was still too dangerous for her to go back to the city because the Japanese were putting all Americans in Manila into prison camps.

Forging a New Identity

While continuing to hide in the hills outside Manila, Phillips undertook her first strike against the Japanese. She heard about a place where they were storing ammunition, and she considered trying to tell John Boone where it was so he could organize troops to blow it up. But Phillips decided to take action herself, and with the help of a few boys also living in the hills, she sneaked down from their hideout and set fire to the ammunition. It soon blew up, destroying the whole supply.

After her successful mission, Phillips was ready to do more to help the war cause. However, in late spring 1942, she came down with malaria and was seriously ill for weeks. She nearly died, but she eventually recovered, only to learn that the American troops had lost some significant battles against the Japanese. American soldiers were being thrown into Japanese prison camps in Manila, and Phillips feared her husband would be among them. She knew she'd have to return to the city to try to find him.

At the end of June, Phillips began the dangerous trip into Manila. She traveled over land and then by boat, hidden under a pile of bananas and coconuts. She knew there was no way for her to be safe unless she concealed her identity as an American. With the help of a Spanish man who worked at the Italian Embassy, she managed to get fake identity papers that said she was Italian. When the papers were ready, she had to get them stamped and signed by a Japanese official. The official asked her to promise she would not help the enemy. "Keeping my fingers firmly crossed ... I promised, and the papers were signed," wrote Phillips in her autobiography.[2]

The Tsubaki Club

With her new papers identifying her as Dorothy Fuentes, Phillips was able to move freely around Manila. Her goal was to help the American soldiers, including her husband, by sending supplies, food, and medicine to the troops being held in the Japanese camps. She also wanted to help John Boone and the soldiers hiding out in the hills. To make money, she decided to return to her job as a nightclub singer. But after a few months working at someone else's club, Phillips realized it would be much better if she had her own club.

She was able to get a loan from a Chinese restaurant owner, and in October 1942, Phillips opened her own nightclub. Located near the harbor where military ships docked, the Tsubaki Club became an instant hit. Phillips made sure everyone knew this was a fancy club and only high-level Japanese military officers would be welcome there.

The decision to open her own club was a very good one. Phillips made a great deal of money, and she was able to buy food and supplies for the American prisoners. There was another important and unexpected benefit: the Japanese military men who came to the club did not worry about talking about military secrets in front of Phillips and the other entertainers at the club. Phillips quickly discovered that she was overhearing information that could be used by the American military forces.

High Pockets the Spy

Before she could do anything with the information she was learning, she got some bad news. Phillips met a German priest who was allowed to visit the prison camps where American soldiers were being held. She asked the priest to try to find her husband and take him some food and clothing. Two weeks later, the priest telephoned: John had died of malaria in late July in the prison camp where he had been held. She was devastated by this news. All along, she had believed she would be reunited with John when the war was over.

The news of John's death made Phillips more determined than ever to help the soldiers in the camps. She also made plans to get the military information she was learning at her club to John Boone.

Ann Dvorak (*center*) plays Claire Phillips in the 1951 film *I Was an American Spy*, which dramatized Phillips's war experiences. This scene takes places in the Tsubaki Club, where Japanese army leaders dined and sometimes shared secret information.

Soon after a profitable holiday season at the Tsubaki Club, Phillips sent some money to Boone along with a note that read, "Our new show a sellout. You can count on regular backing. Standing by for orders and assignments."[3] She signed the note "High Pockets," a nickname she picked because she had begun hiding notes and money in her bra. Boone sent back a message saying that the most important thing he needed was a radio. He could use the radio to communicate with other troops hiding out in the hills. The information might even reach General Douglas MacArthur, the leader of the American troops in the Pacific.

Along with information, Phillips began sending food, clothes, shoes, and soap to Boone and the troops he had working for him. To prevent messages from being discovered, the messengers would "split the center banana in a bunch, put a message inside, and fasten

Speaking in Code

While gathering information to help the Americans, Phillips also continued to send food and money to the men in the prison camps. She began working with a network of other Americans and Filipinos who were running their own operations to help the prisoners. They set up codes to signal each other. If there were letters ready to be smuggled into the camps, they would call each other and say, "Bring your recipes. I'm going to bake today."[4] They had code names for each other, and in case the Japanese were eavesdropping, they spoke in American slang or pig latin to disguise their real plans. This could easily throw off listeners who weren't fluent English speakers.

the skin back into place."[5] Eventually Phillips also managed to find a radio transmitter and sent it to Boone one piece at a time. Once the radio was put together, Boone began transmitting the information Phillips had overheard at the club.

Boone's messages reached General MacArthur, and he would send messages back with new instructions for Phillips. One message asked her to find out what she could about an aircraft carrier docked in the harbor in Manila. Phillips befriended the captain of the Japanese ship and was able to find out when he was leaving and where the ship was headed. When she passed this information to Boone, she knew American forces would probably destroy the ship. Because she liked the Japanese captain, "[She] even cried real tears when he left, as [she] knew [she] was sending him to his doom ... but war is war."[6]

Captured and Tortured

Phillips's operations continued to go smoothly until mid-May 1944, when members of her network were arrested one after another. Phillips knew she might be next, and friends suggested that she should hide in the hills with Boone's troops. She later wrote, "I felt that I owed it to the memory of my [husband] to remain and help his former comrades, regardless of any serious consequences to myself."[7]

On May 23, her resolve was put to the test when four Japanese police officers came to her door. They searched the rooms in her apartment and the office of the Tsubaki Club and told her she would have to go with them. Telling her young daughter that she would be home soon, Phillips was dragged away. She was thrown in a cell, blindfolded, questioned about her activities, and hit or kicked if she didn't provide the answer the Japanese officers were looking for.

Given very little food and water, covered with fleas and lice, bitten by rats, packed into cells with other prisoners, and tortured over and over again, Phillips barely survived her first few months in prison. By August, the prison guards were trying anything they could to get her to talk. One day they tied her to a bench, shoved a hose in her mouth, then turned on the water. Phillips tried to hold her breath but they punched her in the stomach and the water gushed down her throat. She passed out, but her captors woke her by putting burning cigars on her legs. Finally, one day, they told Phillips she was going to be executed. They put her in a guillotine and lowered

the blade onto her neck. "This is it" thought Phillips, and then she "mercifully blacked out."[8] But it was just another attempt to get her to talk.

General Douglas Macarthur (*second from left*) walks to shore with other US Army officers and Filipino military leaders on his return to the Philippines in 1944.

Claire Phillips dines here with David Diamond, who produced *I Was an American Spy*, the 1951 film version of Phillips's memoir about her experiences in the Philippines during the war.

In late September, guards came to get Phillips. She believed she was going to be released but was instead taken to a courtroom. Forced to plead guilty to being a spy, Phillips was sentenced to death. She wasn't afraid because she "figured that death would bring a speedy end to my seemingly endless ordeal of starvation, torture, and illness."[9] However, once again, Phillips's life was spared, and she was moved to a new prison and sentenced to twelve years of hard labor.

Leaving the Philippines

Finally, after more than eight months in captivity, Phillips was rescued by American troops on February 10, 1945. When she saw the troops, she could barely believe her eyes. She ran up to a soldier and touched his arm to make sure she wasn't imagining him. Phillips was soon reunited with her daughter, Dian, and they were finally able to return together to the United States after their long ordeal. As they sailed out of the harbor in Manila, she thought of how she had arrived four years earlier, never imagining all the things that would happen to her.

After the war, the movie *I Was an American Spy* captured Phillips's war adventures. In 1951, Claire Phillips was awarded the Medal of Freedom for her service to her country. She died in 1960 at age fifty-two.

The Countess of Romanones

Aline Griffith lived an exciting life that took her from the world of high fashion to the dangerous work of espionage, from the suburbs of New York to high society in Madrid. Griffith was a model, author, and spy who worked for the OSS and, later on, for the CIA. She had a vibrant social life and was very well connected—her social circle included such celebrities as Elizabeth Taylor, Jackie Kennedy, and Audrey Hepburn. In 1947, Griffith married the Count of Quintanilla and became a Spanish countess, and much of the information she gathered as a spy in the years after the war came from socializing with the Spanish aristocracy in her position as countess. Few people expected that such a fashionable and seemingly high-class socialite would be a spy, but that's exactly how Griffith was able to do her job and help her country.

Joining the OSS

Griffith was born on May 22, 1923, in Pearl River, New York, a small town just north of the border between New York and New Jersey. After college, she began work as a fashion model, but she was soon recruited by the American government. At a dinner party in September 1943, Griffith mentioned to another guest her desire to help in the war effort. She told the man that one of her

In 1947, Aline Griffith married the Count of Quintanilla, after meeting him in Spain, where she'd been assigned by the OSS in 1943. Here, Griffith poses in her home in Madrid in 1964.

brothers was a fighter pilot flying in Europe and another brother was serving on a submarine in the Pacific. She had been hoping to do something to help the United States in the war and was yearning for an adventure. The man at the party said he might be able to help her with both goals.

Just a few weeks later, Griffith received a phone call instructing her to report to Washington, DC. She was told to use a false name, leave her identification at home, and not tell anyone where she was going. Once in Washington, Griffith was given the code name "Tiger" and was sent for training to a location known as the Farm, in the countryside near Washington.

At the Farm, Griffith learned to crack safes and pick locks; she was taught how to make invisible ink and even how to use a folded newspaper as a weapon. Along with the other recruits—all of whom were men—she was put through endless obstacle courses, practiced hand-to-hand combat techniques, and learned to use various weapons. The future spies learned to read maps and use Morse code. They also went on practice missions where they were assigned to follow people and avoid being followed themselves. Griffith and her fellow recruits worked for twenty-one days straight before they got their first day off.

Operation Bullfight

After her grueling training, Griffith's first assignment was in Spain. To prepare, she studied the history, politics, and geography of Spain. She learned that although Spain was officially neutral, many US officials suspected that the country was helping Hitler. The OSS believed that someone in Madrid was giving Allied information to Germany. The

President Franklin Delano Roosevelt established the OSS via presidential military order on June 13, 1942.

The Office of Strategic Services

Formed in June 1942, six months after the bombing of Pearl Harbor, the Office of Strategic Services (OSS) was the primary American intelligence agency during World War II. Prior to the creation of the OSS, various branches of the US government conducted covert operations, but they were very disorganized, so the OSS was formed to coordinate these intelligence activities across the American government and military. Its design was based on the two main British intelligence agencies, the Special Operations Executive (SOE) and the Secret Intelligence Service (SIS). The OSS was dissolved soon after World War II ended, but it was succeeded by the CIA, which is still in operation today.

OSS had a list of four suspects, and it wanted Griffith to find out which one was the traitor.

Operation Bullfight, as Griffith's mission was known, began with a flight to Spain. Griffith had told friends and family that she was going to Spain to work at the American Oil Mission, a real company that was being used as a cover for OSS spies in Madrid. Soon after Griffith arrived, she witnessed a man being murdered in a casino. When she discovered that the man was a fellow agent, she knew her mission was for real. It would be as dangerous as it was important.

Once she reported to work at the American Oil Mission, she learned that her boss there was actually a fellow agent. At their first meeting, he explained Operation Bullfight, which involved getting information to help the Allies with their planned invasion of Germany from the south. Their other mission was to find the double agent working for Germany. After he finished, he cautioned her, saying, "Miss Griffith, if you do not follow orders strictly, you could be responsible for hundreds—or thousands—of deaths of American soldiers."[1]

A Socialite in Madrid

Every day, Griffith reported to work, supposedly for the American Oil Mission. Instead, during the day she was reading coded secret messages from all over the world. After work, she had a second and perhaps more important job. She was assigned to attend parties and get to know people in Madrid. The OSS thought Griffith would be able to get information from these people without them ever suspecting she was a spy.

To help her gather information, Griffith recruited a network of Spanish women. She began her chain of informants with the woman who was helping her improve her Spanish. This woman recruited another woman, who found one more. Eventually, there were fifteen links in this chain of information. Each woman would know only the woman who hired her and the woman she hired; this would protect the whole chain. These women carried messages and gathered information helpful to the Allies. One woman paid a high price for her work with Griffith's network: she was shot to death while sleeping in Griffith's bed while Griffith was away for the weekend. Upon discovering the dead woman when she returned, Griffith realized she was the real target of the bullet. She knew that whoever murdered the woman might come back for her.

Things were getting more dangerous in Madrid. In addition to the murder of Griffith's informant, several agents

48

were murdered. There was also an attempted assassination of Francisco Franco, the leader of Spain, at a bullfight. With the situation in Spain reaching a boiling point, her superiors gave Griffith a pill called an "L pill." The pill was loaded with poison and would kill her instantly if she bit it. She would have to use it if captured so that she could avoid being tortured into giving up secret information.

While Griffith continued to do her OSS work from her base at the American Oil Mission, she continued to attend parties and events around Madrid. She became close with important government connections in Spain and other European countries. At the same time, none of her friends knew that she was a spy. Coincidentally, the father of one of her friends was a German prince living in Madrid. Prince Lilienthal, who was not in favor of Nazi aggression, had important information that he wanted to pass to the Americans, and he suspected Griffith might be able to help.

The prince told Griffith that he believed someone in her office was spying for the Germans. Griffith didn't know who the double agent might be, and of course she could not discuss it with anyone in her office. After all, any one of her coworkers could be the double agent. She contacted her "handler" in Washington, who told her to keep her eyes and ears open. Griffith did just that, but she was in for more danger.

Fact and Fiction

Eventually, Griffith and her fellow agents were able to uncover the identity of the double agent working for the OSS. Once the agent was identified, Griffith and her colleagues developed a plan for her to give him

Aline Griffith is shown here at a gala in Seville on October 28, 2011.
Griffith passed away in December 2017 at the age of ninety-four.

incorrect information about Allied military plans. This false information threw the Germans off track, and they were unprepared for an Allied invasion of Saint Tropez, France. As a result, the invasion proceeded smoothly and was successful.

Griffith continued to work for the OSS in Spain until the end of World War II. After the war, she did some more espionage work in France and Switzerland until retiring from the OSS in 1947. That same year, she married a Spanish count in Madrid and became Aline, Countess of Romanones, and they had three children together before he passed away in 1987.

After her husband's death, Griffith went on to write a number of thrilling memoirs about her work as a spy both during World War II and her further espionage missions in the 1960s and 1970s, when she worked for the CIA. It's not clear how accurate these memoirs are—British historian Rupert Allason claimed that Griffith's accounts of her covert activities were "completely fictional."[2] But Griffith maintained that they were all at least based on truth and argued that her missions were too secretive for anyone not immediately involved to know the truth. Regardless of whether or not the small details of her exploits are factual, Griffith was an important source of information for the US government in the 1940s and beyond.

Code Name Cynthia

Amy Elizabeth Thorpe, later known as Betty Pack and known sometimes in her espionage work as "Cynthia," was a charismatic, adventurous spy who worked for both British and American intelligence agencies in countries across the world. Described as tall, blonde, and willowy, Pack's primary method of gathering information was through romantic relationships. She would seduce an important mark and then, once he had his guard down, Pack would fish for secrets that might help the British and American governments. One of her most significant contributions to the war effort was her work gathering intelligence in Poland that helped the British crack the Enigma machine, which the Germans used to send coded messages. Through her sharp intelligence and deep loyalty to the Allied cause, Pack managed to complete dangerous, daring missions and gather key information that would eventually help the Allies win the war.

An Early Life of Adventure

From the time she was born in Minneapolis, Minnesota, in 1910, Amy Elizabeth Thorpe was on the go. Her father was a captain in the United States Marines, and his job took him to Cuba, Hawaii, Maine, Rhode Island,

and Washington, DC. Known to her family as Elizabeth (although she was later called Betty), she spent much of her time alone, observing the people and places she visited. When her father retired in 1923, the family traveled throughout Europe. There, Elizabeth learned to speak French, and she loved the adventure of travel. When her family returned to Washington, DC, the following year, she missed Europe greatly.

When she was nineteen, Elizabeth met Arthur Pack, a much older British diplomat. A few months later, in April 1930, they were married. Pack was four months pregnant at the wedding, which was considered incredibly scandalous, so the couple moved abroad, and the baby was sent to a foster home soon after being born.

In the early years of their marriage, the couple lived in New York, Chile, England, and Spain. While they were living in Spain in 1936, the Spanish Civil War was raging. It is suspected that Elizabeth Pack may have begun her work as a spy for the British government during this time. She helped some soldiers trapped in enemy territory by smuggling them over the border. She loved the danger and excitement of the situation and felt that "she had found her true calling at last."[1]

In Poland with the Secret Intelligence Service

Arthur was transferred to Warsaw, Poland, in 1937. Some historians suspect that he was transferred so that the British Secret Intelligence Service (SIS, also called MI6) could use Elizabeth Pack in Poland. In the winter of 1938, Arthur had a stroke and returned to England to recover. Meanwhile, Pack began an affair with a Polish diplomat, Edward Kulikowski. He told her about Hitler's plans to take over Czechoslovakia.

Two members of the Women's Royal Navy Service operate the Colossus, the first electronic programmable computer, which British code breakers used to crack the German Enigma code with the help of information gathered by Pack and other spies

Pack knew this information would be of great importance, and she passed it to her friend Jack Shelley, the local station commander for the SIS. As she suspected, he and the British government were very interested in her information and formally recruited her to work for the SIS in March 1938. SIS officials in London were pleased to have Pack working for them. They asked her to gather as much information as possible by befriending Polish officials.

One of the first important men she met was Count Michal Lubienski. He had access to government documents, and she knew he would have top-secret information on Poland's dealings with Germany. Pack began an affair with him, and it is believed that one of the most important things she

Breaking the Enigma

The Enigma machine was a cipher machine invented at the end of World War I by German engineer Arthur Scherbius. There were many versions of the machine, but the ones used by Nazi Germany during World War II were particularly complicated; the codes produced were impossible to break unless you knew how the gears had been set when the code was originally written. No matter how many messages the Allies intercepted, they couldn't learn anything about the Germans' plans without cracking the Enigma code. The British assembled thousands of code breakers, including computer scientist Alan Turing and many female mathematicians, to try to break the cipher. They broke many Enigma codes, but the real goal was to create a program that could decrypt any Enigma cipher. They were successful: by 1945, nearly every German Enigma code could be broken by the British within a few days.

learned about was the Enigma machine. The SIS suspected that Poland might know how to break the Enigma code, and they hoped Pack could get information from Lubienski. Pack was able to find out where Polish research on the Enigma was being done, and she confirmed that the Poles were reading Enigma messages. The full extent of her help isn't known for sure because the existence of the Enigma was not even revealed until the 1970s.

The British Security Coordination

With the prospect of war looming, Pack was forced to leave Warsaw in 1938 and return to London. Meanwhile, Arthur had recovered from his stroke, and he and Pack were sent to Czechoslovakia and then to Chile. From there, Pack tried to keep up with what was happening in Poland. She was very worried about the war and missed being involved, and she frequently wrote to the SIS to get more work as an agent. Finally, in June 1940, the War Office in London wrote to tell her they could use her help.

Leaving her husband behind, she sailed for London in early July and began working right away. However, her mission was cut short when her ship arrived in Lisbon, Portugal. There, she got a telegram from Arthur telling her he needed her in Chile. Disappointed, she began the long trip back by boat. While on the boat, she met Paul Fairly, an American who worked for the Office of Naval Intelligence. He told Pack she might be able to help them with spy work. At this point, "she had reached a point where she was not prepared to allow anything to stand in the way of her participation in the fight [against Hitler]."[2]

Finally, in early 1941, Pack was able to return to the excitement of spy work. She sailed from Chile to New

York City, where she was met by Fairly. He gave her a coded letter with a phone number for her to call. Calling the number, she reached John Arthur Reed Pepper. He became her handler for her work with the British Security Coordination (BSC).

America was not yet involved in the war, and the BSC was a little worried that Pack would have trouble working for the British. They asked her if "she felt strongly enough [about ending the war] to work for us in your own country, [to] spy on your fellow Americans and report to us."[3] They warned her to beware of the FBI and further warned her, "If you are caught, we haven't heard of you. You understand that?"[4]

Pack assured the BSC that she could handle the job. She set up house in Washington, DC, and began throwing parties for politicians and diplomats stationed in Washington. Working under the code name Cynthia, Pack completed several assignments for the BSC.

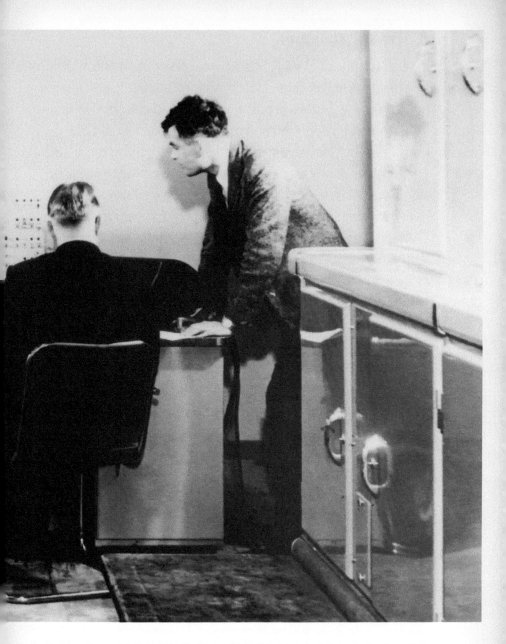

Alan Turing (*far right*), who led the effort to crack the Enigma code, is shown here examining the Ferranti Mark 1 computer with his colleagues. This was the first commercially available computer.

A Spy in Washington

In the spring of 1941, Pack was given a mission that would change her life. Her superiors encouraged her to get to know Charles Brousse, a French diplomat living in Washington. By this time, France had been occupied by the Germans. However, the United States still maintained contact with the Vichy government. Vichy France was the small part of France that Germany allowed to maintain its own government. Although not technically controlled by Germany, in practice the Vichy government cooperated with the Nazis. The British hoped they could prevent Vichy France from falling completely to the Germans. They also hoped to gain valuable information about German plans from French officials.

Pack followed orders and quickly got to know Brousse. Soon they had fallen in love, which did not prevent her from passing any information she got from him to her bosses. Eventually, Brousse began providing information directly to the BSC.

In the spring of 1942, Pack was given her most difficult assignment yet. She was asked to steal the French navy's secret codes (called ciphers) stored in a safe in the French Embassy. These codes would help the Allies decipher secret messages and find out what the French and German plans were well ahead of time. Brousse decided to risk his career to help his lover.

Cracking the Safe

Around the same time, Pack began reporting to the OSS, the new American spy agency. After several months, Pack, her contacts at the OSS, and Brousse finally came up with a plan, and they were ready to put it into action on the

Marshal Philippe Pétain (*right*), president of Vichy France, and Admiral François Darlan (*left*), one of his deputies, are shown here walking down the street with other members of the Vichy government, circa 1940.

night of June 19, 1942. Pack and Brousse had befriended the night watchman at the French Embassy, and he was not surprised to see them there that night. Pack and Brousse invited him to share some champagne with them. They had slipped a knockout drug into his drink, and he quickly fell asleep.

As soon as the watchman was asleep, Pack let in a man known as the Georgia Cracker. He was a safe cracker whom the OSS had had released from prison to do this job, and they felt confident he would be able to pick the lock on the door of the room where the safe was located, as well as the safe itself. However, cracking the safe turned out to be not quite as easy as planned. The early morning hours dragged on with no progress on the safe. By the time they cracked the code to the safe, it was nearly 4:00 a.m., the deadline for when they had to be out of the embassy to avoid being discovered. Tired and disappointed, they had to leave the books in the safe and begin planning another attempt.

The next night, they tried again, but the Georgia Cracker wasn't available. Pack went by herself to the embassy, sneaking past the guard. She attempted to open the safe with the code they'd learned before, but it didn't work. The code had changed.

Third Time's the Charm

Finally, the third time the dangerous plan was put into action, the team was successful. The safe was opened quickly and easily, and the Georgia Cracker slipped out a window with the codebooks. He took them to a nearby hotel room, where a team of photographers waited to take a picture of each page. Pack and Brousse remained in the embassy, worrying the whole time about what would happen if the books did not return on time.

The Georgia Cracker did return with the codebooks, although he was almost forty minutes late. They put the books back in the safe, cleaned up the room, and went to the hotel room where the books had been photographed. According to biographer Mary Lovell, "It seemed as though the entire [room] was filled with tables and photographic equipment, lights, cameras, tripods, cables, and people. But most important were the photographs of the ciphers spread around the room, apparently to dry, on the tables, on the furniture, on the floor."[5] When Pack saw the pictures of the codes, she was struck by the importance of the job she had just accomplished. Historian H. Montgomery Hyde writes, "It was the proudest moment of her life."[6]

Pack and Brousse were congratulated for their completion of the important mission. The photos of the codebooks were flown to England within a day and are said to have saved one hundred thousand lives. There is no way to verify that number, but having the codes certainly helped the Allies. Operation Torch, an Allied invasion of North Africa on November 8, 1942, was aided by the fact that the Allies had the French codes. Colonel Ellery Huntington of the OSS told Pack a few days after the attack that the mission had been a huge success and that it was due to her ciphers. He said, "They have changed the whole course of the war."[7]

A Quiet Life in France

Although this was Pack's most successful mission, it also proved to be her last. The OSS considered sending her to London for more training, but a new plan was developed

This is an example of the Enigma machine used by German forces in World War II. Alan Turing and his colleagues worked to crack the code created by machines like this one.

to send her to France with Brousse. Due to several complications, she and Brousse did not sail to France until October 1944, and by then the war was nearly over.

Once, when asked if she felt shame for how she'd used her sexuality in her spying missions, Pack responded: "Not in the least, my superiors told me that the results of my work saved thousands of British and American lives. It involved me in situations from which 'respectable' women draw back, but mine was total commitment. Wars are not won by respectable methods."[8]

Pack lived the rest of her life in France. She and Brousse divorced their spouses and married, living in a French castle. Pack began writing her memoirs, but she died of cancer in 1963, before she finished writing the story of her life. She didn't think anyone would find her life interesting, but her adventures are still remembered today.

The Celebrated Entertainer

Though many spies were relative unknowns, some were already quite famous and used their fame to help them gather information and travel freely. Josephine Baker was one of these celebrity spies—a well-known singer and dancer in France, Baker traveled throughout Europe and North Africa during the war, carrying secret messages in plain sight. Born in America, Baker first traveled to France as a cabaret performer and quickly became a sensation in Paris.

Baker renounced her American citizenship when she married a Frenchman in 1937, and during World War II she played a significant role in the French Resistance. Because of her fame, Baker was frequently invited to parties with important politicians, and she was able to travel across Europe under the guise of being "on tour," though in actuality she was delivering information to Allied governments. Spies often have to hide who they are, but Baker was successful in her espionage efforts for the opposite reason; her fame provided the perfect disguise.

From Entertainment to Espionage

Baker was born into a poor family in St. Louis, Missouri, in 1906. She got her first job when she was just

Josephine Baker renounced her US citizenship and became a French citizen in 1937. Baker was extremely popular in Paris as an entertainer, and she poses here in a classic stage outfit.

eight years old and worked hard all through her childhood, helping to support her family. By the time she was thirteen, she had found her true calling: dance. She practiced as much as she could and dreamed of one day doing an act onstage.

Her big break came in 1925 when she went to Paris with a dance group. She was a huge hit in France as well as in other European countries. Baker spent the rest of the 1920s touring in Europe before returning to Paris in 1930, where she starred in another show and led a glamorous life. She even had a pet leopard that would walk down the street or take taxis with her. Baker was married briefly in 1937 and continued to live the life of a star. Then war broke out.

Mata Hari

Mata Hari was a famous cabaret dancer who worked as a spy during World War I. Born Margaretha Zelle in the Netherlands, she married a Dutch army captain in 1895 at the age of eighteen and moved to the Dutch East Indies. Their marriage was not a happy one, and Zelle began dancing with an Indonesian troupe and took on the stage name Mata Hari. In 1903, Zelle moved to Paris, where she shot to fame with her cabaret act. When World War I began, Zelle was recruited by the French secret service, who asked her to try to seduce the crown prince of Germany and Prussia in order to obtain German military secrets. The French soon began to suspect that Zelle had started working as a spy for Germany, and in 1917 she was accused of being a double agent and executed by the French government.

When France declared war on Germany in September 1939, Baker was eager to get involved in the war effort. She was not sure how she could help, but the brother of her agent had an idea. He contacted Jacques Abtey, a spy who worked for the French military and was recruiting civilians to help with the war. Abtey wasn't sure Baker would make an ideal spy. He remembered the story of Mata Hari, a famous dancer and spy who had been executed during World War I for spying for the Germans. When he met Baker, Abtey changed his mind. She convinced him that she was very loyal to France and wanted to do anything she could to help.

As a star, Baker had befriended many rich and powerful people in France, people who wouldn't mind telling her things. In fact, in the early days of her spy career, she was so sure she would not be suspected that she wrote information she had obtained on her arms and hands. When warned that this was a dangerous thing to do, she replied, "Oh, nobody would think I'm a spy."[1]

At first, Abtey's fellow spies worried that Baker might not be strong enough for spy work, but Abtey convinced them she was as strong as steel. With her first few missions, she impressed them by being cool in tough situations. She was also endlessly optimistic, assuring them that America would enter the war and the Allies would be sure to win.

From September 1939 to May 1940, Baker gathered information at parties, giving anything she thought might be important to Abtey. During the day, Baker helped people coming to Paris from Belgium in an attempt to escape Hitler.

Like Baker, Mata Hari was a famous cabaret entertainer in Paris who became a spy and used her fame to gather information. She poses here in one of her scandalous performance costumes.

Escaping the Nazi Occupation

When the Germans took over France in June 1940, black people were no longer safe from Hitler, especially in Paris. Even a famous entertainer like Baker could be arrested or killed by Nazis. Baker decided to go to her home in the south of France where the Germans were not yet in control. Abtey eventually joined her there to await their orders for a secret mission.

When their orders came through, Abtey and Baker learned they would be traveling to Portugal to deliver information to an agent there. Before they left, they needed to get the necessary permits and visas that would allow them to travel. For Baker this was easy. Everyone knew her, and it was easy to pretend that she was traveling to Portugal to perform. It was not as easy for Abtey, but he managed to get a fake passport and they were ready to go. All that was left was to figure out how to get the information across the border.

They decided to write it in invisible ink on Baker's sheet music so that they would not need to hide it. In November 1940, they headed to Spain by train and crossed the border easily. No one suspected Baker, and no one even looked at Abtey—they were too busy looking at Baker. Once in Portugal, they took a plane to Lisbon, where Abtey was able to pass the information to his contact.

From North Africa to Spain

Baker and Abtey lived in Algiers in North Africa while awaiting their next assignment. This time, Abtey had trouble getting the paperwork that would allow him to travel. Baker was forced to go alone. Again, she wrote the information in invisible ink on her sheet music. "Who would have guessed it was covered with invisible notations about the [location of the Germans] in southwest France?"[2] she later wrote. She crossed the ocean to Portugal and delivered the information. While she was there, she performed in some shows, went to parties, and gathered more information before returning to Algiers.

Spain was the next stop for Baker. Throughout the spring of 1941, she traveled to major cities in Spain, performing and gathering information along the way. There were many German military officers in Spain, and they were more than happy to talk to the famous and charming Baker. "Being Josephine Baker had definite advantages. Wherever I went I was swamped with invitations," she wrote in her autobiography.[3] She managed to get a great deal of helpful information, which she compiled at the end of the night. "I carefully recorded everything I'd heard," she wrote. "My notes would be highly compromising had they been discovered, but who would dare search Josephine Baker to the skin? The information remained snugly in place, secured [to her underwear] by a safety pin."[4]

The End of a Career in Espionage

Despite all her success, her career as a spy was about to end. In June 1941, she was hospitalized for a severe infection. She remained in the hospital until December 1942 and was so ill that at one point American newspapers reported that she had died. While in the hospital, Baker was not entirely out of the espionage business. Abtey was able to pass information to American military and government officials visiting Baker in the hospital.

Once Baker was finally out of the hospital, she decided to help the war effort in another way. Throughout the rest of

Baker stands at attention in 1961, dressed in her air force lieutenant's uniform, while waiting to receive the Cross of the Legion of Honour, the highest order of merit in the French military.

the war, she performed for Allied troops, trying to boost the morale of the soldiers. The American military officials were happy to have her. In fact, in May 1944, the chief of the air force general staff issued an order to all military officials that they were to use military planes and trucks to help Baker get to her performances.

After the war, Baker's work was recognized by France, who gave her the Medal of Resistance in October 1946. She missed the excitement of the war but married again, adopted twelve children, and traveled and performed all over the world. In the 1950s, she returned to the United States, fighting for civil rights for African Americans. She spoke in front of 200,000 people at the March on Washington for Jobs and Freedom on August 28, 1963, alongside Martin Luther King Jr.

Baker suffered a heart attack in 1973, and after nearly fifty years of performing, she began to slow down. On April 8, 1975, she gave her final performance. Two days later, she died of a stroke. She is remembered today not only as a celebrated entertainer and former agent of the French Resistance, but also as a civil rights activist and a key figure in Jazz Age Paris.

A Writer and a Spy

Mary Bancroft was an American spy, journalist, and intelligence analyst during World War II who became involved with the OSS while she was living in Switzerland. Born in Boston, Massachusetts, on October 29, 1903, Bancroft came from a wealthy family, and she was very close to her step-grandfather, C. W. Barron. He was the publisher of the *Wall Street Journal*, and he encouraged her adventurous spirit and suggested she become a journalist. Later on, she used the skills she'd picked up from Barron to disguise her espionage activities as journalism and in analyzing the Swiss media during the war.

Survival in Switzerland

Bancroft went to Smith College, but immediately after her first year she married Sherwin Badger, and they went to live in Cuba for a year. When they returned to the United States, the couple lived in Boston and then in New York City, where Bancroft wrote some articles for her grandfather's publications, the *Wall Street Journal* and *Barron's*. Bancroft and Badger had two children together, but eventually they divorced when the children were still

C. W. Barron purchased Dow Jones & Company in 1903 and maintained control of the company and the *Wall Street Journal* until his death in 1928.

very young. Soon after her divorce, Bancroft took a boat to Europe, and on her trip met Jean Rufenacht, a Swiss businessman. They married, and Bancroft went to live with him in Zurich, Switzerland.

While living in Zurich during the 1930s, Bancroft watched the beginnings of World War II closely. In 1934, she visited Germany and was scared by what she saw there. Hitler's grip on Germany was growing stronger, and she wasn't sure what would happen. Bancroft was listening to the radio, along with the rest of Europe, as Hitler invaded Czechoslovakia in 1938. She was listening again as England declared war on Germany in September 1939 and continued to listen as country after country was invaded by the Germans.

During the first years of the war, Bancroft and her family were just trying to get by in Switzerland, dealing with shortages of food and heating oil. Soon, Switzerland was completely surrounded by countries that were controlled by the Germans. Although she worried about what might happen to her and her family, she wanted to stay in her adopted country. However, she was also eager to help the United States with the war effort, even if she was not living there. Bancroft was not sure how she could help, but when a man from the United States Embassy called to ask if she would write articles about the war for Swiss and American newspapers, she jumped at the chance to play even a small role.

Working for the OSS

What Bancroft did not know was that the man who had contacted her was really recruiting her to work for the OSS. In December 1942, he introduced her to

Allen Dulles was recruited to a leadership position in the CIA in January 1951 and became director of the organization in 1953. He was dismissed from the position in 1961 by President John F. Kennedy.

Allen Dulles, an American man working at the US Embassy. At first, Bancroft was not aware of who Dulles was, but she soon discovered that he was working on intelligence missions for the OSS.

By January 1943, Bancroft was carrying out small missions for the OSS, working closely with Dulles. Bancroft's work as a journalist provided a good cover for her spy work. She was able to meet lots of people, go to parties, and travel freely. At the end of every week, she would take the train to Bern, Switzerland, where Dulles was based. There, she would turn over information she had gathered that week. Dulles and Bancroft would call intelligence officials in Washington, DC, and issue their report. They knew that the Swiss officials might be listening in on these phone calls, so Bancroft would sometimes slip in false information to throw them off track.

Bancroft was successful in her information-gathering duties. She was fluent in both German and French and was

Allen Dulles

A lawyer turned intelligence analyst, Allen Dulles is best known for being the director of the CIA from 1953 to 1961, during the first decade of the Cold War. Before serving with the CIA, however, Dulles worked with the OSS during World War II, gathering information and coordinating espionage activities in Bern, Switzerland. Though he was married at the time, Dulles was involved in a romantic relationship with Bancroft for much of the time they worked together. Dulles passed away on January 29, 1969, at the age of seventy-five.

able to blend in well with Swiss citizens. Bancroft was also a good listener—a skill that helped her in her journalism and spying duties. She later wrote that she "very quickly learned the value of personal relationships, how important it was to win people's trust and confidence."[1] She knew that developing good sources of information was extremely important. Those initial sources could lead her to their sources, and so on. Bancroft described intelligence work as being like a puzzle, where you must fit all the pieces together. Small pieces of information that might seem to be insignificant could turn out to bring the whole picture into focus.

The Double Agent

After they had worked together a few months, Dulles told Bancroft that he had a much more important project for her. A German military man named Hans Gisevius had been in contact with Dulles and was interested in turning over military information to the Allies. Gisevius worked for the Abwehr, part of the German military. However, Gisevius didn't like the Nazis—not because what they were doing was wrong, but because he thought he was better than them. He came to Switzerland to make contact with the Allies and begin making plans to overthrow Hitler.

Gisevius also wanted Dulles to help him translate into English a book he had written about the Nazis. He wanted to be able to publish it in America as soon as the war was over. Dulles agreed to help Gisevius—and help the OSS while he was at it. Dulles's plan was to have Bancroft do the translation and get any information she could from Gisevius while she was working with him. Dulles told Bancroft, "I want you to report to me everything he says to

Hans Bernd Gisevius was a German diplomat who spied on the Nazi government for the United States and the German Resistance.

you—everything. With you working on his book, he may be off his guard and say things to you that contradict the story he is telling me."[2] Bancroft was nervous about the new job and afraid that she would not be able to handle this large task, but she agreed to take it on.

At their first meeting, Bancroft was surprised to see that Gisevius had brought 1,415 pages of manuscript—and that wasn't even the whole book! Bancroft knew she had to be careful with Gisevius. She thought he might be spying on her, so she could not reveal anything that would be helpful to him. At the same time, she had to gain his trust so that he might tell her things he wouldn't tell Dulles. She also had to keep him happy so that he would continue to help the OSS.

The July 20 Plot

Early in July 1944, Gisevius disappeared suddenly. Bancroft believed he had gone to Germany, but she was not sure what he was doing there. That month, Bancroft went on vacation, taking Gisevius's manuscript with her. On July 20, Bancroft learned of a failed attempt to kill Hitler. But it was not until she returned to Zurich in September that she learned what had happened to Gisevius. Gisevius had been involved in the plot to assassinate Hitler, and she was unsure whether he was alive or dead.

Bancroft finally heard from him in January 1945, but "he looked at least ten years older. His hair had turned gray and he had lost a tremendous amount of weight."[3] At first, Gisevius was too tired to talk, but after a few days his story came pouring out. He and his group had planted a bomb that had gone off but had not killed Hitler. Many other conspirators had been captured and executed, but

In this March 5, 1994, photo, Mary Bancroft sits in her home in New York, holding her third and final book, *Autobiography of a Spy*, which was published by William Morrow in 1983.

Gisevius had escaped, using a fake passport Dulles had arranged to have made and sent to him in Germany.

After the War

When the war in Europe was finally over, Bancroft traveled on various assignments to European countries devastated by the war. In France, she got to see firsthand the destruction of cities, the graves of soldiers, and the people who still didn't have enough food, clothing, or other necessities. Many people looked stunned, even though the real horrors of war were behind them.

Bancroft also went to Nuremberg, Germany, where Nazi leaders were put on trial for their war crimes. She was very interested to see the people she'd written about in the Swiss papers convicted of the horrible things they'd done.

Bancroft returned to the United States in 1953. She lived in New York City and kept in touch with Dulles and Gisevius. Later, Gisevius published *To the Bitter End*, the book that Bancroft had worked so hard to translate. Bancroft also became an author in her own right, publishing two novels and an autobiography.

Bancroft never forgot her war experiences. "World War II ... changed me, my life, my whole outlook on the world. I have never been able to see anything in the same way since."[4] When Bancroft died in January 1997, the *New York Times* recognized her for her "brilliant work in Switzerland in World War II."[5]

Chronology

1903 **October 29** Mary Bancroft is born in Boston, Massachusetts.

1906 **April 6** Virginia Hall is born in Baltimore, Maryland.

June 3 Josephine Baker is born in St. Louis, Missouri.

1907 **December 2** Claire Phillips is born in Portland, Oregon.

1910 **November 22** Elizabeth "Betty" Pack is born in Minneapolis, Minnesota.

1923 **May 22** Aline Griffith is born in Pearl River, New York.

1938 **March** Betty Pack begins working for British SIS in Poland.

1939 **September** Josephine Baker begins working for French military intelligence.

September 1 Germany invades Poland.

September 3 England and France declare war on Germany.

1940 **June 14** France falls to Germany.

November Josephine Baker flees the Nazi occupation of France for Spain.

1941 **June** Josephine Baker is hospitalized and ceases most of her spying activities.

June 22 Germany attempts to invade the Soviet Union.

August Virginia Hall is recruited by the SOE and is sent to France.

September Claire Phillips arrives in Manila, Philippines.

December 7 Japan bombs Pearl Harbor, Hawaii.

December 8 United States declares war on the Axis powers.

1942 June 13 President Franklin Roosevelt establishes the OSS.

June 19–21 Betty Pack steals French naval ciphers from French Embassy.

October Claire Phillips opens the Tsubaki Club and begins her spy operations.

December Mary Bancroft is recruited by the OSS in Switzerland.

1943 September Aline Griffith is recruited by the OSS and sent to Spain.

1944 May 23 Claire Phillips is arrested for spying.

July 20 German military fails in attempt to assassinate Hitler.

1945 February 10 Claire Phillips is rescued from prison by American troops.

April 29 Hitler commits suicide.

May 7 Germany surrenders.

May 8   Victory in Europe is declared by the Allies.

August 6   United States drops atomic bomb on Hiroshima, Japan.

August 9   United States drops atomic bomb on Nagasaki, Japan.

August 14   Victory in the Pacific is declared by the Allies.

September 20   The OSS is dissolved.

Chapter Notes

Introduction

1. Albert Marrin, *The Secret Armies: Spies, Counterspies, and Saboteurs in World War II* (New York: Atheneum, 1985), p. 106.

Chapter 1
The Limping Lady

1. Linda McCarthy, *Spies, Pop Flies, and French Fries: Stories I Told My Favorite Visitors to the CIA Exhibit Center* (Markham, VA: History Is a Hoot, Inc., 1999), p. 45.
2. Margaret L. Rossiter, *Women in the Resistance* (New York: Praeger, 1986), p. 190.
3. Rossiter, p. 191.
4. Elizabeth P. McIntosh, *Sisterhood of Spies: The Women of the OSS* (Annapolis, MD: Naval Institute Press, 1998), p. 114.
5. McCarthy, p. 48.

Chapter 2
An American in the Philippines

1. Claire Phillips, as told to Frederick C. Painton, "I Was an American Spy" (*American Mercury*, May 1945), p. 592.

2. Claire Phillips and Myron B. Goldsmith, *Manila Espionage* (Portland, OR: Binfords & Mort, 1947), p. 82.
3. Phillips and Goldsmith, p. 105.
4. Phillips and Goldsmith, p. 113.
5. Phillips and Painton, p. 594.
6. Phillips and Goldsmith, p. 121.
7. Phillips and Goldsmith, p. 171.
8. Phillips and Goldsmith, p. 198.
9. Phillips and Goldsmith, p. 201.

Chapter 3
The Countess of Romanones

1. Aline, Countess of Romanones, *The Spy Wore Red: My Adventures as an Undercover Agent in World War II* (New York: Random House, 1987), p. 84.
2. Nigel West, *Historical Dictionary of Sexpionage* (Lanham, MD: Scarecrow Press, 2009), p. 326.

Chapter 4
Code Name Cynthia

1. Ernest Volkman, *Spies: The Secret Agents Who Changed the Course of History* (New York: John Wiley & Sons, Inc., 1994), p. 108.
2. Mary S. Lovell, *Cast No Shadow: The Life of the American Spy Who Changed the Course of World War II* (New York: Pantheon Books, 1992), p. 135.

3. Donald Downes, *The Scarlet Thread* (London: Verschoyle, 1953), pp. 59–60.
4. Downes, pp. 59–60.
5. Lovell, p. 229.
6. H. Montgomery Hyde, *Cynthia* (New York: Farrar, Straus and Giroux, 1965), p. 204.
7. Lovell, p. 240.
8. Emily Yellin, *Our Mothers' War: Women at Home and at the Front During World War II* (New York: Free Press, 2004), p. 233.

Chapter 5
The Celebrated Entertainer

1. Jean-Claude Baker and Chris Chase, *Josephine: The Hungry Heart* (New York: Random House, 1993), p. 227.
2. Josephine Baker and Jo Bouillon, *Josephine* (New York: Marlowe & Company, 1977), p. 124.
3. Baker and Bouillon, p. 125.
4. Baker and Bouillon, p. 125.

Chapter 6
A Writer and a Spy

1. Mary Bancroft, *Autobiography of a Spy* (New York: William Morrow and Company, Inc., 1983), p. 150.
2. Bancroft, p. 162.
3. Bancroft, p. 207.

4. Bancroft, pp. 291–292.
5. Elizabeth P. McIntosh, *Sisterhood of Spies: The Women of the OSS* (Annapolis, MD: Naval Institute Press, 1998), p. 182.

Glossary

Allies   The countries that banded together at the start of World War II to oppose the Axis, including France, Poland, the United Kingdom, the United States, and, after Germany's attempted 1941 invasion, the Soviet Union.

amputate   To surgically remove a limb.

assassination   A murder, sometimes carried out for political reasons.

autocrat   A nation's ruler who wields absolute power.

Axis   The countries that fought against the Allies in World War II, including Germany, Italy, and Japan, the three of which originally negotiated diplomatic treaties allowing each to expand its control over Western Europe, Eastern Europe, and Asia, respectively.

cipher   A message in code.

Cold War   A long standoff between the United States and the Soviet Union over nuclear weapons.

conspirators   People who join together to carry out an illegal act.

decrypt   To decode.

diplomat   A person hired to negotiate, or work between, two nations.

embassy   An office or building where diplomats conduct business.

espionage The use of spies to obtain information.

ethnostate A nation or other sovereign state where citizenship is only granted to people who belong to a specific racial or ethnic group.

fascism A form of government that has a one-party dictatorship and opposes democracy.

Gestapo Nazi Germany's secret police.

guillotine A machine with a sharp, heavy blade used to behead people.

malaria A disease caused by parasites, often transmitted by mosquitoes.

Morse code A code using dots or dashes to transfer information.

smuggle To secretly carry goods or information.

Vichy government The French government headed by Philippe Pétain that cooperated with the Nazis in their invasion of France.

Bibliography

Aline, Countess of Romanones. *The Spy Wore Red: My Adventures as an Undercover Agent in World War II.* New York: Random House, 1987.

Baker, Jean-Claude, and Chris Chase. *Josephine: The Hungry Heart.* New York: Random House, 1993.

Baker, Josephine, and Jo Bouillon. *Josephine.* Translated by Mariana Fitzpatrick. New York: Marlowe & Company, 1977.

Bancroft, Mary. *Autobiography of a Spy.* New York: William Morrow and Company, Inc., 1983.

Blum, Howard. *The Last Goodnight: A World War II Story of Espionage, Adventure, and Betrayal.* New York: Harper, 2016

Breuer, William B. *The Great Raid on Cabanatuan: Rescuing the Doomed Ghosts of Bataan and Corregidor.* New York: John Wiley & Sons, 1994.

Central Intelligence Agency. "The Office of Strategic Services: America's First Intelligence Agency." 2016. Retrieved March 22, 2019. https://www.cia.gov/library/publications/intelligence-history/oss.

Gruhzit-Hoyt, Olga. *They Also Served: American Women in World War II.* New York: Carol Publishing Group, 1995.

Hyde, H. Montgomery. *Cynthia.* New York: Farrar, Straus and Giroux, 1965.

Kaminski, Theresa. *Prisoners in Paradise: American Women in the Wartime South Pacific.* Lawrence, KS: University Press of Kansas, 2000.

Lovell, Mary S. *Cast No Shadow: The Life of the American Spy Who Changed the Course of World War II.* New York: Pantheon Books, 1992.

Mahoney, M. H. *Women in Espionage: A Biographical Dictionary.* Santa Barbara, CA: ABC-CLIO, Inc., 1993.

Marrin, Albert. *The Secret Armies: Spies, Counterspies, and Saboteurs in World War II.* New York: Atheneum, 1985.

McCarthy, Linda. *Spies, Pop Flies, and French Fries: Stories I Told My Favorite Visitors to the CIA Exhibit Center.* Markham, VA: History Is a Hoot, Inc., 1999.

McIntosh, Elizabeth P. *Sisterhood of Spies: The Women of the OSS.* Annapolis, MD: Naval Institute Press, 1998.

Melton, H. Keith. *The Ultimate Spy Book.* New York: DK Publishing, Inc., 1996.

Mulrine, Anna. "The Power of Secrets." *U.S. News and World Report,* January 27–February 3, 2003, pp. 48–49.

O'Toole, G. J. A. *Honorable Treachery: A History of U.S. Intelligence, Espionage, and Covert Action from the American Revolution to the CIA.* New York: The Atlantic Monthly Press, 1991.

Phillips, Claire, and Myron B. Goldsmith. *Manila Espionage.* Portland, OR: Binfords & Mort, 1947.

Phillips, Claire, as told to Frederick C. Painton. "I Was an American Spy." *American Mercury* 60, May 1945, pp. 592–598.

Rose, Phyllis. *Jazz Cleopatra: Josephine Baker in Her Time.* New York: Doubleday, 1989.

Rossiter, Margaret L. *Women in the Resistance.* New York: Praeger, 1986.

Rowan, Richard Wilmer, with Robert G. Deindorfer. *Secret Service: Thirty-Three Centuries of Espionage.* New York: Hawthorn Books, Inc., 1967.

Sheehan, Sean. *WWII: Germany and Japan Attack.* Austin, TX: Raintree/Steck-Vaughn Publishers, 2001.

Sides, Hampton. *Ghost Soldiers: The Forgotten Epic Story of World War II's Most Dramatic Mission.* New York: Doubleday, 2001.

Singer, Kurt. *Spy Stories from Asia.* New York: Wilfred Funk, Inc., 1955.

Smith, R. Harris. *OSS: The Secret History of America's First Central Intelligence Agency.* Berkeley, CA: The University of California Press, 1972.

Sullivan, George. *In the Line of Fire: Eight Women War Spies.* New York: Scholastic, Inc., 1996.

Vail, John J. *World War II: The War in Europe.* San Diego: Lucent Books, 1991.

Volkman, Ernest. *Spies: The Secret Agents Who Changed the Course of History.* New York: John Wiley & Sons, Inc., 1994.

West, Nigel. *Historical Dictionary of Sexspionage.* Lanham, MD: Scarecrow Press, 2009.

Yellin, Emily. *Our Mothers' War: Women at Home and at the Front During World War II.* New York: Free Press, 2004.

Further Reading

Books

Atwood, Kathryn J. *Women Heroes of World War II: 32 Stories of Espionage, Sabotage, Resistance, and Rescue.* 2nd ed. Chicago, IL: Chicago Review Press, 2019.

Barlow, Col. Cassie, and Sue Norrod. *Saluting Our Grandmas: Women of World War II.* Gretna, LA: Pelican Publishing, 2017.

Caravantes, Peggy. *The Many Faces of Josephine Baker: Dancer, Singer, Activist, Spy.* Reprint edition. Chicago, IL: Chicago Review Press, 2018.

Mitchell, Don. *The Lady Is a Spy: Virginia Hall, World War II Hero of the French Resistance.* New York, NY: Scholastic Nonfiction, 2019.

Mundy, Lisa. *Code Girls: The True Story of the American Women Who Secretly Broke Codes in World War II.* Young Readers Edition. New York, NY: Little, Brown Books for Young Readers, 2018.

Websites

International Spy Museum

www.spymuseum.org

The International Spy Museum, located in Washington, DC, has numerous resources on its website, including a spying dictionary and *SpyCast*, a podcast that features interviews with real spies and espionage experts.

National Women's History Museum

www.womenshistory.org

The website for the National Women's History Museum in Alexandria, Virginia, offers digitized exhibits, articles, and other resources about women throughout American history.

National World War II Museum

www.nationalww2museum.org

The National World War II Museum is a museum located in New Orleans, Louisiana, dedicated to showcasing the history of the United States' involvement in World War II. Its website includes student resources, profiles on key figures, and the ability to search its collections.

Index